FOSTER YOUR *LIFE*

HAYLEY FOSTER

ISBN: 978-0-578-41379-2

All graphics designed by Katie Bray | www.katielbray.com

FOSTER YOUR *LIFE*

HAYLEY FOSTER

To all of the women in my life that continue to inspire me, motivate me and give me the support to do what I truly love to do. I thank YOU with all my heart and soul.

To my supportive, loving and understanding husband and children and my beautiful mixed-up modern family... thank you for all that you do, all the love you give and all the support you provide to make my life feel full and absolutely complete.

A MOMENT OF GRATITUDE MAKES A DIFFERENCE IN ATTITUDE

Creating this workbook is something I had initially wanted to do even before I put pen to paper on *Foster Your Passion*. However, I needed to go through the process of writing my first book before I could put together an accompanying workbook.

The beautiful women in my 12-Week Fostering program inspired me to move forward with the workbook after the few weeks of using the mocked-up journals I had created for them. They told me how inspired they were by the quotes, how it guided them, gave them strength, motivation and inspiration to keep on pushing forward. They found themselves digging deeper into their feelings and shifting their mindsets towards positivity and their focus on success.

My hope is that you will find a new version of yourself and will move your business or life to a new level by the time you land on the last page of this book.

I'd love to hear your feedback, your insights and your success stories from using *Foster Your Life*. Please share them with me at passion@fostering101.com or post them on Social Media @fostering101.

ABOUT THIS WORKBOOK

Welcome to the Foster Your Life Workbook. The story behind this book is quite simple. After writing Foster Your Passion, so many people asked me why I didn't leave more space so they can write more in the FosterU sections.

Over the years, I have found many journals filled with hundreds of pages of motivation quotes - as you may know, I am obsessed with quotes - that I continue to use throughout my business. A few months ago, I began my 12-Week Fostering Group - a program designed to move women along on their journey by providing them structure, guidance, support, motivation, accountability and reflection - both personally and professionally. I longed to provide them with an accountability tool to give them structure and thought-provoking questions to help them dig deeper into their visions and shift their mindsets. I began to pull quotes that matched my content for the course and my book and so became, *Foster Your Life* - A 12-week guide to motivate, inspire and change your life.

Before you begin, I ask that you make a commitment to using this book and not just let it sit in a pile and accumulate dust. Below are the agreements I ask you to make with yourself because the only person that can change you, is YOU. If you agree, put your initials next to each one.

_____ I will strive for progress, not perfection

_____ I will take responsibility for my commitments, my actions and my decisions

_____ I will use an accountability partner and check in weekly (enter their name here) _____.

_____ I will step outside my comfort zone and commit to goals that help me 'stretch' myself

_____ I will spend 10-20 minutes reviewing last week's progress and the current weeks action plan on Sunday night or Monday morning to ensure my week is focused

_____ I will use my calendar to block time each day for strategic time to complete my tasks that focus on my 12-week plan.

_____ I will go to _____ (person's name) for support

_____ I will strive to have a positive mindset for the next 12 weeks

Now that we're on the same page, let's go FOSTER YOUR LIFE!

fos·ter

/ˈfôstər,ˈfästər/
verb

*encourage or promote
the development of
something good*

LET'S START WITH *you...*

Name: _____

What is the most important or meaningful thing about
yourself that you want others to know?

_____

_____

_____

_____

_____

_____

_____

_____

_____

_____

_____

_____

_____

_____

TELL ME, WHAT IS IT
YOU PLAN TO DO
WITH THIS ONE

wild AND

precious

life?

—Mary Oliver

What journey are you on? What do you want out of life?

_____

_____

_____

_____

_____

_____

_____

_____

_____

_____

_____

_____

_____

Visualize it. See it! Believe it! Make it happen!

LEARN BY *doing,* BY *failing,* AND BY GETTING BACK UP AND *trying* AGAIN.

List three experiences that have had the most impact on who you are as a person and how they've changed you and made you better than you were before.

_____

_____

_____

_____

_____

_____

_____

_____

_____

_____

_____

_____

_____

_____

_____

_____

_____

happiness

IS A

journey

NOT A

destination

Thinking happy thoughts, makes you a happier person. Even just saying to yourself *'Today I'm going to be Happy'* can change your mindset.

Close your eyes and think about what makes you smile and lights you up inside. List as many things as you can on this page that make you truly happy. Be neat... be messy... be whatever makes you happy.

_____

_____

_____

_____

_____

_____

_____

_____

_____

_____

_____

_____

_____

_____

DO MORE OF WHAT

LIGHTS

YOU UP

AND SETS YOUR

SOUL ON

fire

Look at the list on the last page of the things in your life that light you up, fill you up and make you feel alive. How can you incorporate at least one of these into your week this week?

_____

_____

_____

_____

_____

_____

On the flip side, list the things in life that make you feel unhappy. Deflated. Defeated. Burned out. How can you remove at least one of these from your week this week?

_____

_____

_____

_____

_____

_____

IF YOU WANT TO GO FAST,

go alone.

IF YOU WANT TO GO FAR,

go together.

- AFRICAN PROVERB

Who are your biggest fans? Who do you go to or will you go to for support - emotional, financial, educational, motivational? List your tribe below and what type of support they will provide you.

1. _____

_____

_____

_____

2. _____

_____

_____

_____

3. _____

_____

_____

_____

4. _____

_____

_____

_____

5. _____

_____

_____

_____

Behind every successful woman is a **TRIBE** of other successful women that have her back

Go through your database of contacts. Who can help you achieve your goals and who might you be able to help achieve theirs. Be a selfless connector. It will come back around.

_____

_____

_____

_____

_____

_____

_____

_____

_____

_____

_____

_____

_____

_____

_____

Be You!

everyone else
is already taken

-Oscar Wilde

How would people describe you? Who is the person you aspire to be? Write down your 3 core values... your fundamental beliefs that define you as a person or as a business.

1. _____

2. _____

3. _____

If you have trouble with the above, reach out to your tribe and ask 12 of them to help you out by sending you three words they feel best describes you as a person or as it relates to your business. Pick the most popular 3 words and use them above.

Then write about a time when you were (pick one from above).

_____

_____

_____

_____

_____

_____

_____

THE MEANING OF *life,* IS TO GIVE LIFE *meaning*

What inspired you to start doing what you do? Why do you do what you do? When you start with WHY, you are making an emotional connection with your customer in order to get them to know, like and trust you. Your Why is also what gives you/your life meaning and purpose.

What's your 'WHY'?

_____

_____

_____

_____

_____

_____

_____

_____

_____

_____

_____

_____

_____

_____

Wherever you go, go with all your heart

What do you want to achieve in life? Fill in single word answers for each of the ones below. On the right side of the page, on a scale of 1 - 10, rank them as to where you feel you are at this moment in your life compared to where you want to be.

RANKING

Business:

Personal:

Financial:

Emotional:

Physical:

LET'S SET SOME *goals*

Everyone needs a goal or how else would you know where you want to go in life. When it comes to setting goals, there is a standard that millions of people swear by, it's called "SMART Goal Setting".

S - Specific
What do I want to achieve?
How am I going to do it?
What do I want the end result to be?

M - Measurable
How will I know I've reached my goal?
Is there a metric that will tell me?
Like a number on a scale or a change in your Instagram following.

A - Achievable
Can I see myself doing this?
What are some of the tasks I need to do to get it done?

R - Realistic
Is the goal too big, lofty or too difficult?
Or is it too easy and lacking challenge?

T - Timely
When do I want to accomplish it by?

If you *fail to plan* you may as well *plan to fail*

Make sure that you equip yourself with the tools you need to achieve your goals. Here are my top tools for your toolkit:

#1 - **Faith** - Believe in Yourself

#2 - **Support** - Find Your People, those that will support you on your mission

#3 - **Inspiration** - Look to others who inspire you and hopefully the words and pages in this book will do the trick

#4 - **Motivation** - Reward yourself along your journey

Now... Let's Set Some Goals!

YOU ARE NEVER
TOO OLD
TO SET ANOTHER
GOAL,
OR TO DREAM
A NEW
DREAM.

-C.S. LEWIS

Where do you want to be 12 weeks from today? What changes do you want to make...

	In your life?	In your business?
1.	_____	_____
	_____	_____
	_____	_____
2.	_____	_____
	_____	_____
	_____	_____
3.	_____	_____
	_____	_____
	_____	_____
4.	_____	_____
	_____	_____
	_____	_____
5.	_____	_____
	_____	_____
	_____	_____

MAKE SHIT HAPPEN

What do you need to get you there? Is it money, more clients, more support, education, motivation, accountability?

_____

_____

_____

_____

_____

_____

_____

Why do you want to make these changes in your life? What will change for you if you make them?

_____

_____

_____

_____

_____

_____

BE
BRAVE.
TAKE
CHANCES.
EXPERIENCE
EVERYTHING.
JUST DO IT.

Outside our comfort zone is where the magic happens. It's where we grow! What scares you? What makes you uncomfortable? What you can do to step outside your comfort zone.

_____

_____

_____

_____

_____

_____

_____

_____

I plan to _____

in the next 12 weeks by doing _____

_____

I will ask _____ to hold me accountable to this or I will share it on social media so that I am publicly held accountable.

Learn

FROM THE PAST.

Live

IN THE PRESENT.

Believe

IN THE FUTURE.

What have you learned from the past 3-6 months in life or in your business?

_____

_____

_____

_____

What's working?

_____

_____

_____

What's not working?

_____

_____

_____

What can you do differently?

_____

_____

_____

A goal

without a plan
is just

a wish

Write down 3-5 goals that you want to achieve in the next 12 weeks.

1. ———————————————————————

———————————————————————

———————————————————————

2. ———————————————————————

———————————————————————

———————————————————————

3. ———————————————————————

———————————————————————

———————————————————————

4. ———————————————————————

———————————————————————

———————————————————————

5. ———————————————————————

———————————————————————

———————————————————————

You cannot wait for the **STORM** to pass, you must learn to **DANCE** in the **RAIN**

What are some possible challenges you think you might face to achieve those goals. List them below and how you believe you can overcome them.

Challenge: _____

Solution: _____

_____

_____

Challenge: _____

Solution: _____

_____

_____

Challenge: _____

Solution: _____

_____

_____

Make something of all that *wishful* thinking

Go back to your goals you listed a few pages back. Write down your GOAL and list 3-5 action items you need to do in order to achieve this goal.

GOAL #1:

Action Items:

1. _____

_____

_____

_____

2. _____

_____

_____

_____

3. _____

_____

_____

_____

4. _____

_____

_____

Dream
Big. Be
Grateful.
Love
Hard.

GOAL #2:

Action Items:

1. _____

_____

_____

2. _____

_____

_____

3. _____

_____

_____

4. _____

_____

_____

5. _____

_____

_____

When people
are determined,
they can
overcome

anything.

-*Nelson Mandela*

GOAL #3:

Action Items:

1. _____

_____

_____

_____

2. _____

_____

_____

_____

3. _____

_____

_____

_____

4. _____

_____

_____

_____

5. _____

_____

_____

WHEN YOU
love
WHAT YOU *have,*
YOU HAVE
everything
you need.

GOAL #4:

Action Items:

1. _____

_____

_____

_____

2. _____

_____

_____

_____

3. _____

_____

_____

_____

4. _____

_____

_____

_____

5. _____

_____

_____

Life isn't about finding yourself. Life is about creating yourself.

GOAL #5:

Action Items:

1. _____

   _____

   _____

   _____

2. _____

   _____

   _____

   _____

3. _____

   _____

   _____

   _____

4. _____

   _____

   _____

   _____

5. _____

   _____

   _____

YOU CAN'T *see* WHAT'S AHEAD, IF YOU DON'T TAKE THE FIRST STEP *forward*

What is ONE thing you can do TODAY to get you started on each of your goals?

Goal #1:

_____

_____

Goal #2:

_____

_____

Goal #3:

_____

_____

Goal #4:

_____

_____

Goal #5:

_____

_____

WEEK
one

Today is the *first* day of the rest of your life

DATE: _____

Today starts Day 1 of your 12 Week Journey!

How are you feeling about what's ahead? Are you excited? Nervous? Anxious? Overwhelmed? Write it down.

_____

_____

_____

_____

_____

_____

_____

_____

_____

_____

_____

_____

WE CANNOT *DISCOVER* NEW *OCEANS* UNLESS WE HAVE THE *COURAGE* TO LOSE SIGHT OF THE *SHORE*

Week #1 Focus:

_____

_____

_____

List 3-5 tactics you must do this week

	To do	By When
1.	_____	_____
	_____	_____
	_____	_____
2.	_____	_____
	_____	_____
	_____	_____
3.	_____	_____
	_____	_____
	_____	_____
4.	_____	_____
	_____	_____
	_____	_____
5.	_____	_____
	_____	_____
	_____	_____

Life doesn't have to be perfect *to be* beautiful

How will you reward yourself on this journey? Write down something you can do or give yourself each week for a job well done.

1._____   7._____

2._____   8._____

3._____   9._____

4._____   10._____

5._____   11._____

6._____   12._____

Write below your 'Bigger' rewards for achieving your 'Bigger' goals. Like a car or a grand vacation or an experience.

1. _____

2. _____

3. _____

4. _____

5. _____

YOU MUST BE THE
change
YOU WISH TO
see
IN THE WORLD

-NELSON MANDELA

What can you say 'Yes' to that you've been saying 'No' to?

_____

_____

_____

_____

_____

_____

_____

_____

What can you say 'No' to that you've been saying 'Yes' to?

_____

_____

_____

_____

_____

_____

_____

ENJOY

THE

LITTLE

THINGS

Look around you... take in the little things. What do you see day to day that makes you smile? Open your mind to seeing more beauty in the world this week. Write your findings below.

_____

_____

_____

_____

_____

_____

_____

_____

_____

_____

_____

_____

_____

_____

_____

EVERYTHING IN
LIFE IS A
REFLECTION OF
A CHOICE YOU
HAVE MADE. IF YOU
WANT A DIFFERENT
RESULT, MAKE
A DIFFERENT
CHOICE

Weekly Reflection: Reflect back on the week.

Where did you get stuck?

_____

_____

What can you do differently?

_____

_____

What came easily to you?

_____

_____

What were your big wins?

_____

_____

_____

On a scale of 1 - 10, how would you rank your week in terms of focus, prioritizing, happiness, accomplishing tasks?

Weekly Ranking: _____

LIVE EACH DAY WITH

grace,

love &

laughter

Weekly Notes, Doodles, Insights, Brain Dump:

WEEK

two

Always look on the **bright** side of life

Week #2 Focus:

_____

_____

_____

List 3-5 tactics you must do this week

To do	By When

1._____   _____

_____   _____

_____   _____

2._____   _____

_____   _____

_____   _____

3._____   _____

_____   _____

_____   _____

4._____   _____

_____   _____

_____   _____

5._____   _____

_____   _____

_____   _____

MAY YOUR
JOY
BE AS
DEEP
AS THE
OCEAN

A Week of JOY

Do one thing every day this week that brings you JOY. Even if it's just a little thing. Share it below.

Monday: _____

_____

Tuesday: _____

_____

Wednesday: _____

_____

Thursday: _____

_____

Friday: _____

_____

Saturday: _____

_____

Sunday: _____

_____

beauty begins the moment you decide to be yourself

-COCO CHANEL

What makes you YOU? On the left side: List your skills, strengths, values, qualities, likes. On the right side: list your dislikes, weaknesses, bad habits/qualities. Be honest about who you are.

The Good: The Not So Good:

_____   _____

_____   _____

_____   _____

_____   _____

_____   _____

_____   _____

_____   _____

_____   _____

_____   _____

_____   _____

_____   _____

_____   _____

_____   _____

Good people
bring out
the *good*
in people

Write down all of the good things that have happened to you this past week, month or year.

_____

_____

_____

_____

_____

_____

_____

_____

_____

_____

_____

_____

_____

_____

_____

_____

_____

_____

_____

LIFE
IS
beautiful

OPEN YOUR EYES TO
MAKE SURE YOU SEE
THE BEAUTY IN IT

Weekly Reflection: Reflect back on the week.

Where did you get stuck?

_____

_____

What can you do differently?

_____

_____

What came easily to you?

_____

_____

What were your big wins?

_____

_____

_____

On a scale of 1 - 10, how would you rank your week in terms of focus, prioritizing, happiness, accomplishing tasks?

Weekly Ranking: _____

KEEP IT SIMPLE.

KEEP IT HONEST.

KEEP IT *REAL.*

Weekly Notes, Doodles, Insights, Brain Dump:

WEEK

three

The happiest people
don't have the
best of everything.
They just

make

the best
of everything.

Week #3 Focus:

_____

_____

_____

List 3-5 tactics you must do this week

To do	By When

1._____ _____

_____ _____

_____ _____

2._____ _____

_____ _____

_____ _____

3._____ _____

_____ _____

_____ _____

4._____ _____

_____ _____

5._____ _____

_____ _____

ENJOY EVERY MOMENT OF

life

A Week of Gratitude

Journal each morning this week with one thing you are grateful for. You can even get your family or friends in on the fun and have them make a list as well.

Monday: _____

_____

_____

Tuesday: _____

_____

_____

Wednesday: _____

_____

_____

Thursday: _____

_____

_____

Friday: _____

_____

_____

Saturday: _____

_____

_____

Sunday: _____

_____

ASK YOURSELF IF
WHAT YOU ARE DOING
today
IS GETTING YOU CLOSER
TO WHERE YOU WANT *TO BE*
tomorrow

FOCUS: *Follow One Course Until Success*

What does it look like when you are in your zone, focused and grinding?

_____

_____

_____

_____

List out the things that distract you and get in your way?

_____

_____

_____

_____

Write down a few actionable steps you can take to keep your focus and stay in your zone.

_____

_____

_____

_____

CHASE YOUR DREAMS...

YOU JUST MIGHT CATCH THEM

What do you aspire to be? What are your dreams in life?

_____

_____

_____

_____

_____

_____

_____

How would your life be different if you were to accomplish them?

_____

_____

_____

_____

_____

_____

_____

YOU HAVE THE POTENTIAL TO MAKE

beautiful things

Weekly Reflection: Reflect back on the week.

Where did you get stuck?

_____

_____

What can you do differently?

_____

_____

What came easily to you?

_____

_____

What were your big wins?

_____

_____

_____

On a scale of 1 - 10, how would you rank your week in terms of focus, prioritizing, happiness, accomplishing tasks?

Weekly Ranking: _____

Color
outside
the
lines

Weekly Notes, Doodles, Insights, Brain Dump:

_____

_____

_____

_____

_____

_____

_____

_____

_____

_____

_____

_____

_____

_____

_____

_____

_____

_____

_____

WEEK

four

DO WHAT MAKES
YOUR HEART SING.

inspire

OTHERS.

inspire

YOURSELF.

Week #4 Focus:

_____

_____

_____

List 3-5 tactics you must do this week

	To do	By When
1.	_____	_____
	_____	_____
	_____	_____
2.	_____	_____
	_____	_____
	_____	_____
3.	_____	_____
	_____	_____
	_____	_____
4.	_____	_____
	_____	_____
	_____	_____
5.	_____	_____
	_____	_____
	_____	_____

NO ONE
is in charge
of your
happiness,
except
YOU

A Week of YOU

What are some things that you can do for yourself this week? Maybe it's booking a business conference or course you've been wanting to take or a small thing that you've been neglecting like a manicure, massage or getting your hair done.

Monday: _____

_____

Tuesday: _____

_____

Wednesday: _____

_____

Thursday: _____

_____

Friday: _____

_____

Saturday: _____

_____

Sunday: _____

_____

EVERYTHING YOU CAN IMAGINE IS

real

-PABLO PICASSO

List 3 – 5 things that you can improve moving into the next 4 weeks. What actions can you take to improve them?

Item	Action
1._____	_____
_____	_____
_____	_____
2._____	_____
_____	_____
_____	_____
3._____	_____
_____	_____
_____	_____
4._____	_____
_____	_____
_____	_____
5._____	_____
_____	_____
_____	_____

WE CAN CHANGE THE WORLD.
IT IS IN YOUR HANDS TO MAKE A

difference.

-NELSON MANDELA

What have you changed about yourself or your business in the past 4 weeks?

_____

_____

_____

_____

_____

_____

_____

How do these changes make you feel?

_____

_____

_____

_____

_____

_____

_____

SOME PEOPLE

dream

OF SUCCESS

WHILE OTHERS
WAKE UP &

work
hard

FOR IT

Weekly Reflection: Reflect back on the week.

Where did you get stuck?

_____

_____

What can you do differently?

_____

_____

What came easily to you?

_____

_____

What were your big wins?

_____

_____

_____

On a scale of 1 - 10, how would you rank your week in terms of focus, prioritizing, happiness, accomplishing tasks?

Weekly Ranking: _____

Ideas, Plans, Hopes & Dreams

Weekly Notes, Doodles, Insights, Brain Dump:

WEEK
five

Not all those who *Wander* are lost

-J.R.R. Tolkien

Week #5 Focus:

_____

_____

_____

List 3-5 tactics you must do this week

To do	By When

1._____   _____

_____

_____

2._____   _____

_____

_____

3._____   _____

_____

_____

4._____   _____

_____

_____

5._____   _____

_____

_____

Enjoy More / Complain Less

Believe More / Doubt Less

Relax More / Worry Less

Focus More / Wander Less

What can you do MORE of and LESS of this week or in your life in general? List at least 3 - 5 examples like the ones on the left.

_____

_____

_____

_____

_____

_____

_____

_____

_____

_____

_____

_____

_____

_____

_____

_____

_____

_____

Our fingerprints don't fade from the *lives we touch.*

- Maya Angelou

Write Your Legacy: What do you want to leave behind?
How do you want to be remembered?

_____

_____

_____

_____

_____

_____

_____

_____

_____

_____

_____

_____

_____

_____

_____

_____

_____

_____

all
you
need
is
love

-The Beatles

Write about a time when you are 'Loving' life or what you do for work. Imagine yourself in that moment. Write about it.

_____

_____

_____

_____

_____

_____

_____

Write about a time when you are 'Not Loving' what you do for work, feeling frustrated, annoyed, burnt out. Write about it below.

_____

_____

_____

_____

_____

_____

AMAZING THINGS CAN HAPPEN... WHEN YOU *trust* YOUR *gut*

Weekly Reflection: Reflect back on the week.

Where did you get stuck?

_____

_____

What can you do differently?

_____

_____

What came easily to you?

_____

_____

What were your big wins?

_____

_____

_____

On a scale of 1 - 10, how would you rank your week in terms of focus, prioritizing, happiness, accomplishing tasks?

Weekly Ranking: _____

Choose your own PATH

Weekly Notes, Doodles, Insights, Brain Dump:

_____

_____

_____

_____

_____

_____

_____

_____

_____

_____

_____

_____

_____

_____

_____

_____

_____

_____

_____

WEEK

six

IT'S NOT HOW FAR YOU
ARE FROM REACHING
YOUR GOAL, BUT HOW
FAR YOU'VE COME
FROM WHERE YOU
FIRST STARTED!

Week #6 Focus:

_____

_____

_____

List 3-5 tactics you must do this week

To do   By When

1._____   _____

_____   _____

_____   _____

2._____   _____

_____   _____

_____   _____

3._____   _____

_____   _____

_____   _____

4._____   _____

_____   _____

_____   _____

5._____   _____

_____   _____

_____   _____

DO WHAT YOU

love.

LOVE WHAT

you do.

What can you delegate in your life/business?

_____

_____

_____

_____

_____

_____

_____

_____

What can you or should you automate?

_____

_____

_____

_____

_____

_____

_____

A positive
attitude
will lead to
positive
outcomes

-Nelson Mandela

This is Week 6... You're half-way there! What changes have you made that you're proud of?

_____

_____

_____

_____

_____

_____

_____

_____

What changes do you still need/want to make in your life/business?

_____

_____

_____

_____

_____

_____

_____

Yesterday is history.

Tomorrow is a mystery.

Today is God's gift.

That's why we call

it the PRESENT.

How can you be more 'Present' this year?

_____

_____

_____

_____

In Business?

_____

_____

_____

With Family?

_____

_____

_____

In Your Relationship?

_____

_____

_____

THINK DEEPLY

LIVE KINDLY

LOVE TRULY

DANCE FREELY

SPEAK GENTLY

LAUGH DAILY

Weekly Reflection: Reflect back on the week.

Where did you get stuck?

_____

_____

What can you do differently?

_____

_____

What came easily to you?

_____

_____

What were your big wins?

_____

_____

_____

On a scale of 1 - 10, how would you rank your week in terms of focus, prioritizing, happiness, accomplishing tasks?

Weekly Ranking: _____

BE YOUR OWN *HERO*

Weekly Notes, Doodles, Insights, Brain Dump:

WEEK
seven

LIVE IN THE
sunshine.
SWIM IN THE
sea.
DRINK THE WILD
air.

Week #7 Focus:

_____

_____

_____

List 3-5 tactics you must do this week

	To do	By When
1.	_____	_____
	_____	_____
	_____	_____
2.	_____	_____
	_____	_____
	_____	_____
3.	_____	_____
	_____	_____
	_____	_____
4.	_____	_____
	_____	_____
	_____	_____
5.	_____	_____
	_____	_____
	_____	_____

Don't put off tomorrow what you can do today.

Today *is the* day.

Do one thing each day this week that you've been putting off for the last 6 weeks or longer. Make it a point to dedicate at least 5 minutes to getting it started.

When we start something, our brain is trained to get us to actually finish it

Monday: _____

_____

Tuesday: _____

_____

Wednesday: _____

_____

Thursday: _____

_____

Friday: _____

_____

Saturday: _____

_____

Sunday: _____

_____

NO MATTER WHAT PEOPLE TELL YOU, WORDS AND IDEAS CAN CHANGE *the world*

— ROBIN WILLIAMS

What can you share with your friends or your tribe this week that has worked for you. Inspired you. Motivated you. Helped you. It can be a website, book, app, etc. Make a list below of your favorites or share it on Social Media.

_____

_____

_____

_____

_____

_____

_____

_____

_____

_____

_____

_____

_____

why fit in, when you were born to stand out!

Authenticity is knowing who you are and being brave enough to live it. What does it look like when you are your most AUTHENTIC self?

_____

_____

_____

_____

_____

_____

_____

_____

_____

_____

_____

_____

_____

_____

_____

_____

THE BEST WAY
TO PREDICT
THE FUTURE,
IS TO
invent it

Weekly Reflection: Reflect back on the week.

Where did you get stuck?

_____

_____

What can you do differently?

_____

_____

What came easily to you?

_____

_____

What were your big wins?

_____

_____

_____

On a scale of 1 - 10, how would you rank your week in terms of focus, prioritizing, happiness, accomplishing tasks?

Weekly Ranking: _____

Weekly Notes, Doodles, Insights, Brain Dump:

WEEK
eight

"Believe in Yourself"

said your heart to your brain

Week #8 Focus:

_____

_____

_____

List 3-5 tactics you must do this week

	To do	By When
1.	_____	_____
	_____	_____
	_____	_____
2.	_____	_____
	_____	_____
	_____	_____
3.	_____	_____
	_____	_____
	_____	_____
4.	_____	_____
	_____	_____
	_____	_____
5.	_____	_____
	_____	_____
	_____	_____

Leave a little *kindness* wherever you go

Weekly Kindness Challenge

Go out of your way this week to do one thing each day that is 'Kind'. Get your family, friends, community in on it. Share it with others. Encourage them to try it.

Monday: _____

_____

Tuesday: _____

_____

Wednesday: _____

_____

Thursday: _____

_____

Friday: _____

_____

Saturday: _____

_____

Sunday: _____

_____

strength

-AND-

growth

COME ONLY THROUGH
CONTINUOUS EFFORT
AND STRUGGLE

- NAPOLEON HILL

What does 'GROWTH' mean for you or for your business? From a personal growth perspective does it mean being more mindful? More spiritual? More open-minded? For your business, does it mean more clients? More money? More staff? More office space?

_____

_____

_____

_____

_____

_____

_____

_____

_____

_____

_____

_____

_____

YOU CANNOT
CHANGE THE
DIRECTION OF
THE WIND,
BUT YOU CAN

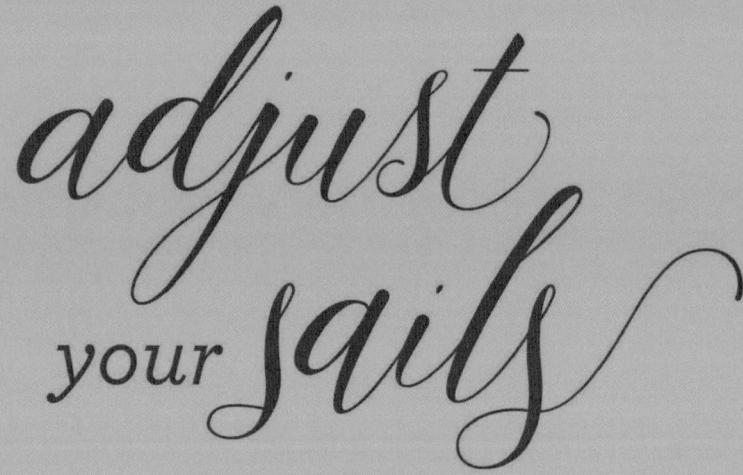

adjust
your sails

Think about something in your life that has been hard or challenging. Instead of feeling like it happened 'TO YOU', change your language to say it happened 'FOR YOU'.

Write about how you've grown from it.

_____

_____

_____

_____

_____

_____

_____

_____

_____

_____

_____

_____

_____

_____

_____

_____

Learn
FROM YESTERDAY,

live
FOR TODAY,

hope
FOR TOMORROW.

-ALBERT EINSTEIN

Weekly Reflection: Reflect back on the week.

Where did you get stuck?

_____

_____

What can you do differently?

_____

_____

What came easily to you?

_____

_____

What were your big wins?

_____

_____

_____

On a scale of 1 - 10, how would you rank your week in terms of focus, prioritizing, happiness, accomplishing tasks?

Weekly Ranking: _____

TODAY

IS

MY

GREATEST

adventure

Weekly Notes, Doodles, Insights, Brain Dump:

_____

_____

_____

_____

_____

_____

_____

_____

_____

_____

_____

_____

_____

_____

_____

_____

_____

_____

_____

WEEK

nine

GOOD THINGS COME TO THOSE WHO

wait

BUT THE

best

THINGS COME TO THOSE WHO

do!

Week #9 Focus:

_____

_____

_____

List 3-5 tactics you must do this week

	To do	By When
1.	_____	_____
	_____	_____
	_____	_____
2.	_____	_____
	_____	_____
	_____	_____
3.	_____	_____
	_____	_____
	_____	_____
4.	_____	_____
	_____	_____
	_____	_____
5.	_____	_____
	_____	_____
	_____	_____

It always
seems
impossible
until it
is done.

- Nelson Mandela

Commit to doing something every day this week that challenges you. Check off below for each day you did it. Then reward yourself if you did it every day.

M____ T____ W____ Th____ F____ S____ S____

Monday: _____

_____

Tuesday: _____

_____

Wednesday: _____

_____

Thursday: _____

_____

Friday: _____

_____

Saturday: _____

_____

Sunday: _____

_____

We shape our

DESTINY

if we follow the direction of our

DREAMS

What has felt 'impossible' or challenging but once you did it, you realized that it wasn't all that bad. Write about it.

Don't
quit
your
day
DREAM

Have you been thinking about another business you'd like to start or have you found something that really lights you up and gets you going, outside of your normal day job? When people act on this itch they get, we call it the 'Side Hustle'. Write about something below that you might want to start doing on the side.

_____

_____

_____

_____

_____

_____

_____

_____

_____

_____

_____

_____

_____

_____

THE WORLD
IS YOUR
oyster

Weekly Reflection: Reflect back on the week.

Where did you get stuck?

_____

_____

What can you do differently?

_____

_____

What came easily to you?

_____

_____

What were your big wins?

_____

_____

_____

On a scale of 1 - 10, how would you rank your week in terms of focus, prioritizing, happiness, accomplishing tasks?

Weekly Ranking: _____

PUT THE
MAP DOWN
AND GET

wonderfully

LOST

Weekly Notes, Doodles, Insights, Brain Dump:

WEEK

ten

STRIVE FOR

balance

AND YOU
WILL FIND

harmony

Week #10 Focus:

_____

_____

_____

List 3-5 tactics you must do this week

To do	By When
1._____	_____
_____	_____
_____	_____
2._____	_____
_____	_____
_____	_____
3._____	_____
_____	_____
_____	_____
4._____	_____
_____	_____
_____	_____
5._____	_____
_____	_____
_____	_____

CHANGE YOUR

words,

CHANGE YOUR

mindset

This week, instead of saying: 'I have to', say 'I Get To' and instead of 'I can't' say, 'I can'.

I'm in
love with
cities
i've never
been to and

people

i've never met.

It's all about SUPPORT. Who can help you go far in life/business? Write their names below and how you can connect with them. Maybe it's a call or a coffee or a message.

_____

_____

_____

_____

_____

_____

_____

_____

_____

_____

_____

_____

_____

_____

_____

_____

_____

live every day with intention.

With 3 weeks to go, set your intentions for the rest of the book. Make sure they are Meaningful, Attainable, Positive! Use these intentions to map your plan for the next 3 weeks.

_____

_____

_____

_____

_____

_____

_____

_____

_____

_____

_____

_____

_____

_____

_____

FOREVER
IS
COMPOSED
OF
NOWS

Weekly Reflection: Reflect back on the week.

Where did you get stuck?

_____

_____

What can you do differently?

_____

_____

What came easily to you?

_____

_____

What were your big wins?

_____

_____

_____

On a scale of 1 - 10, how would you rank your week in terms of focus, prioritizing, happiness, accomplishing tasks?

Weekly Ranking: _____

LIFE IS

full

OF

POSSIBILITIES

Weekly Notes, Doodles, Insights, Brain Dump:

WEEK
eleven

do

small

things

with

great

love

— MOTHER TERESA

Week #11 Focus:

_____

_____

_____

List 3-5 tactics you must do this week

	To do	By When
1.	_____	_____
	_____	_____
	_____	_____
2.	_____	_____
	_____	_____
	_____	_____
3.	_____	_____
	_____	_____
	_____	_____
4.	_____	_____
	_____	_____
	_____	_____
5.	_____	_____
	_____	_____
	_____	_____

EVERY
SINGLE
DAY DO
SOMETHING
THAT MAKES
YOUR HEART
sing

-MARCIA WIEDER

How will you reward yourself daily this week with something that makes you happy/makes your heart sing?

Monday: _____

_____

Tuesday: _____

_____

Wednesday: _____

_____

Thursday: _____

_____

Friday: _____

_____

Saturday: _____

_____

Sunday: _____

_____

EVERYTHING BEGINS WITH AN

IDEA

Write down 3 big ideas you can bring into your business or life in the next 12 weeks.

1. _____

_____

_____

_____

_____

2. _____

_____

_____

_____

_____

3. _____

_____

_____

_____

_____

Dream the Impossible.

Seek the Unknown.

Achieve *Greatness.*

Write a letter to yourself from the person you want to be 12 months from now. Talk about where you are, how you got there and what you had to overcome.

_____

_____

_____

_____

_____

_____

_____

_____

_____

_____

_____

_____

_____

_____

_____

_____

_____

_____

_____

Creativity

— TAKES —

Courage

- HENRI MATISSE

Weekly Reflection: Reflect back on the week.

Where did you get stuck?

_____

_____

What can you do differently?

_____

_____

What came easily to you?

_____

_____

What were your big wins?

_____

_____

_____

On a scale of 1 - 10, how would you rank your week in terms of focus, prioritizing, happiness, accomplishing tasks?

Weekly Ranking: _____

Be Crazy
and Dream
but

never

Be Boring

Weekly Notes, Doodles, Insights, Brain Dump:

WEEK
twelve

A winner is a dreamer who *never* gives up

- Nelson Mandela

Week #12 Focus:

_____

_____

_____

List 3-5 tactics you must do this week

To do	By When

1._____   _____

_____   _____

_____   _____

2._____   _____

_____   _____

_____   _____

3._____   _____

_____   _____

4._____   _____

_____   _____

5._____   _____

_____   _____

THERE IS

always

A REASON
TO

smile

What has changed for you since Week 1?

	RANKING	
	Wk 1	Wk 12

Business:

Personal:

Financial:

Emotional:

Physical:

WE STRIVE
FOR
progress,
NOT
perfection

Reflect back on the past 12 weeks. What have you accomplished? What has made you proud of yourself?

_____

_____

_____

_____

_____

_____

_____

_____

_____

_____

_____

_____

_____

_____

_____

_____

_____

_____

IF YOU CAN
imagine it,
YOU CAN
create it.
IF YOU CAN
dream it,
YOU CAN
become it.

What did you learn about yourself in the past 12 weeks
that you didn't think when you started this program?

_____

_____

_____

_____

_____

_____

_____

_____

_____

_____

_____

_____

_____

_____

_____

_____

_____

_____

Dream
BIG.
Sparkle
MORE.
Shine
BRIGHTER.

Looking back at your goals from the first week, what have you achieved?

_____

_____

_____

_____

_____

_____

_____

_____

_____

_____

What do you still have to achieve moving forward?

_____

_____

_____

_____

_____

_____

_____

THAT'S A *wrap!*

A MOMENT
OF
gratitude
MAKES A
DIFFERENCE IN
attitude

State of the Union:

Below is a ranking of key categories that impact your day to day life. Fill them in accordingly. Use the following to rank your status:

1. Stuck, Drained
2. Unmotivated, Indecisive
3. Comfortable, Status Quo
4. Inspired, Ready for more
5. Excited, Booming

Pillar		Rank	Working	Not Working	To Do
Personal	Week 1:				
	Week 4:				
	Week 8:				
	Week 12:				
Business	Week 1:				
	Week 4:				
	Week 8:				
	Week 12:				
Relationship	Week 1:				
	Week 4:				
	Week 8:				
	Week 12:				

Pillar		Rank	Working	Not Working	To Do
Health	Week 1:				
	Week 4:				
	Week 8:				
	Week 12:				
Financial	Week 1:				
	Week 4:				
	Week 8:				
	Week 12:				
Spiritual	Week 1:				
	Week 4:				
	Week 8:				
	Week 12:				

ABOUT THE AUTHOR

Hayley Foster is the Chief Fostering Officer of Foster Inc., an entrepreneur many times over, podcast host of Foster Your Passion podcast, and a published author of *Foster Your Passion*.

In addition to Foster Inc., Hayley has also built an online platform for women to share their personal stories to help them connect on a more meaningful level with other women entrepreneurs at FosterWomen.com.

Hayley runs a series of workshops through her FosterU division and plans to take Foster Your Passion workshops on the road. If you would like to schedule a workshop in your city, you can email passion@fostering101.com.

Since this book has been self-published, if you would like to order in bulk for your team, your school or your group, we can save you a fortune. Please reach out to passion@fostering101.com.

You can find Hayley on all social channels at @fostering101.

Hayley lives in Port Washington, New York—the city she believes to be the entrepreneurial capital of Long Island, with her entrepreneurial husband, Brian, and her two daughters, Marley and Jackson, and stepson, Sebastian.

Made in the USA
Coppell, TX
07 January 2022